I0419468

How to Write a Non-Fiction Kindle eBook

Step-by-Step Guide to Writing a Non-Fiction eBook that Sells!

By

Michele Gilbert

Visit My Amazon Author Page

Dedicated to those who choose to stretch beyond their own limits and to seek a more abundant and fulfilling life.

Your thoughts are creative.

Michele Gilbert

Table of contents

Introduction

First, I want to thank you and congratulate you for downloading the book, "How to Write a Non-Fiction Kindle eBook."

I believe that *everyone* has a book to write and a story to tell regardless of their level of education, writing ability, or perceived 'exciting-ness' of their lives.

Let's take **you** for example.

Your life is completely unique.

You have a distinct set of personal experiences and memories.

Your DNA and fingerprints identify *only you* to such an extent that these pieces of evidence are pivotal in criminal cases.

Most important, you are the only one with *your heart, your passions, and the ability to express those to the world.*

Unfortunately, when it comes to writing a book, many people feel like they have nothing to say.

To make matters worse, they worry about self-criticism and the criticisms of others.

They worry about starting but never finishing.

They worry about finishing and publishing a book that no one reads or that people read and hate.

They even worry about success and how becoming a successful author might negatively impact their lives through extra stress, no privacy, and a previously non-existent responsibility to spread the message.

Beyond these worries and fears lies a much deeper, more sinister problem.

That problem is low self-esteem.

The dictionary defines esteem as "respect and admiration, typically for a person."

Thus, maintaining low self-esteem implies that you are disrespecting and even scorning your body, mind, or spirit.

In my opinion, since I believe *everyone* has a book to write and a story to tell, the fact that you have bought this short book indicates that you're finally ready to turn an eye inward, pay attention to what's inside, and honor what you find by expressing it to the world.

In other words, whether you know it consciously, you've finally made the decision to elevate your self-esteem.

And I couldn't be more excited to help you in this transformative, life-changing process!

The goal of what's in these pages is to not only help you tap into the pool of intense desire and enthusiasm that *already exists within you,* but also provide you with a time-tested method of 'Putting that Passion on the Page and Publishing the Product.'

If you read and complete the effective exercises and examples laid out in this short book, you will learn *in 25 minutes or less* how to write down your lessons, words of wisdom, and personal experiences in a readable, profitable format.

Furthermore, you will immediately raise your self-confidence and –esteem because you will see just how easily the words flow out of you. You will watch in amazement as your book develops before your eyes.

And, you'll start to realize just how valuable this information is to other people.

Your first book is just the beginning of a 6- or 7-figure information business.

The objective is to find that niche group that responds to what you're writing (and is willing to pay you money for more of your time and information.)

But, don't take my word for it.

This graph from authorearnings.com demonstrates that 20% of the money generated from Amazon's best-selling e-books are from independent or single-author publishers.

The kicker is that these statistics represent only 40% of Amazon's total e-book revenue because 60% comes from the non-best-selling e-books. For the average e-book, independent and single-author publishers are not only more common, but rake in a higher percentage of the total revenue.

With these hard facts in mind, I promise that if you take the time to read this book and complete the exercises, you will have a powerful product that will both claim a portion of Amazon's ever-growing e-book revenue stream and serve as the foundation for a larger 6- or 7-figure information empire.

But, I need to warn against a half-assed attempt at this project.

In order for you to respect and admire that intense, burning source of enthusiasm inside of you, you need to give it your full attention and effort.

John Wooden described true success in this area of your life as "peace of mind which is a direct result of self-satisfaction in knowing you did your best to become the best you are capable of becoming."

No one is looking over your shoulder keeping tabs on whether you are giving your 100% best effort.

No one can hold you accountable *except yourself.*

You need to prioritize that self-satisfaction over the opinion of others…

…For at least the next 48 hours of your life. That's all I'm asking.

The first step in this process is for you to continue reading *right now, while you're thinking about it.*

Get started *today* so that you can live the lifestyle you deserve tomorrow.

See you on the next page.

CHAPTER 1: Researching Your Topic

"Give me six hours to chop down a tree and I will spend the first four sharpening the axe." ~Abraham Lincoln

Before we jump into the tools and tricks available for you to determine the viability and profitability of your forthcoming book, we first need to discover the topic of the book that's *already waiting inside you* to be written.

Imagine that the content of your book is like water at the bottom of a well.

In the middle of the vast landscape of your mind, you have this well sticking out, begging to be tapped and explored, filled with fresh, vital water, but currently inaccessible.

Luckily, the first exercise in this book is like the bucket that you can lower into the well and pull out some of the water.

Exercise #1: Stream-Of-Consciousness Topic Generator

1) Open a new Word Document.
2) Save the title as 'What I Love To Write About'
3) Set a timer for 5 minutes.
4) Write down *everything* that pops into your mind no matter how ridiculous or seemingly 'un-writable.'
5) When the timer finishes, go back through and highlight the top 3 choices.
6) Find anything else in the document that relates to these 3 topics.
   a. Group the information into 3 clusters. It's ok if there is overlap, you can list something in two or more clusters if it fits.

If at any point you stop writing because you can't think of another topic, start typing about what you're noticing.

"I've stopped writing. Can't think of anything. Pushing myself to keep writing and keep thinking of topics. I hear birds chirping outside... Oh the different bird calls could be interesting. Or how sounds affect the brain. Binaural beats and music and vibrational energy. I remember reading about cymatics..."

The primary benefit and goal of this stream-of-consciousness exercise is to remove your 'thinking brain' from the process of discovery.

Said simply, your routine thoughts, opinions, and assumptions are what have held you back from writing this book *that's already within you.*

They have pushed the water, that vital source of intense passion and wisdom, beneath the surface of your daily consciousness. That's why the original analogy involves a well, and why you need this exercise, the bucket, to retrieve what has been buried.

A common mistake when performing this exercise is editing and criticizing every idea that appears on the page. You want each thing you write down to be 'publishable' and 'sensible.'

But, again, the goal of this exercise is to take everything that's been stored inside you and put it all on the page in one quick burst, no matter how idiotic or insulting.

Think about opening up a can of Coca-Cola.

The first few seconds involve an intense burst of energy as the carbonation explodes through the narrow opening. After the initial eruption, the soda calms down and settles into a delicious drink.

The same can be said about what's been welling up inside of you.

When you first sit down to perform this exercise, there will be an eruption of ideas, possibilities, tangential concepts, quotes, and memories that are all competing to get onto the page.

You'll find that the limitation is how fast you can type.

That is, however, unless you let your self-criticisms act as an extra barrier that stops these integral parts of yourself from surfacing.

Now, if this happens and you find yourself unable to complete the exercise at first, that's ok. In fact, it's totally normal.

Remember that for the past however-many-years you've been suppressing and over-looking these integral parts of yourself. You've been routinely practicing low self-esteem.

And I don't say that to be critical or mean or to encourage you to beat yourself up for it…

Instead, my hope is that you will actually go easy on yourself if you happen to run into this troubling reality.

You will see, perhaps for the first time, the consequences of your habitual thinking patterns. It's akin to looking in the mirror after years of poor eating habits and truly waking up to the consequences that have accumulated after hundreds of bad, but routine, dietary decisions.

In other words, the problem is not specific to *you*. You are not different in the sense of being helpless, irreparable, or having no hope.

The problem afflicts the majority of the population. Again, I believe *everyone* has a book to write and story to tell, but how many of the people you know have actually expressed their well of wondrous words?

Assessing the Contents, Demand and Profitability of Your Book

Now that you have these 3 core topics, there are 2 free, fantastic online tools to help you flesh out the specifics of what you're writing about, and another 2 that will help you determine whether people actually want to read what you have to write.

Free Research Resource #1: Wikipedia

Wikipedia represents a great launching point for an author's forthcoming project.

The open-source encyclopedia is free, constantly updated, and brimming with relevant information regarding your particular topic.

Best of all, the page contains a list of 'related searched' and 'references' for further exploration.

Free Research Resource #2: Web Google Searches

Compared to other search engines like Yahoo or Bing!, Google maintains the most sophisticated algorithms to determine what articles and information should rank for particular search terms.

The benefit of Google's expensive indexing and filtering systems is that the most relevant, useful articles typically appear on the first page of your search.

Thus, you can quickly research a topic by looking through Google's first page of search results.

Another interesting feature is that Google displays the number of 'total results' for a given search term. With this information, you can quickly determine whether your topic has either a broad audience or a broad set of people publishing content.

Top 5 Research Tips

1) **Research one topic at a time.** The blessing and the curse of the Internet is that everything is easily, instantly accessible. Make sure you stay focused and on-topic during this process.
2) **Create separate documents for each topic.** Make sure there is a sharp distinction to avoid confusion. Again, if there is overlap you can paste information into two or more pages.

3) Keep track of where you find information. In the central document for each topic, make sure you list the URLs, article titles, and key points in an organized fashion. That way, you can not only quickly scan your unified research document to remember what you found, but you can re-access each article easily without dealing with the frustration of 'where did I get this from?' and retracing your steps to find the source.

4) Copy and paste. When performing research, save time by copy/pasting the URL, title, and article highlights. Avoid rewriting the content as you go. In this way, you will condense all the relevant information on the Internet exactly as it's presented into one document.

5) Separate the 'Research Phase' from the 'Writing Phase.' Many writers are uncomfortable with the concept of copy/paste because they aren't creating original content. In other words, they feel weird 'lifting' someone else's information. By separating research from writing, however, you ensure that this first *phase* of the writing process is neither the finished product nor even a first draft. Instead, by strictly copy/pasting, you give yourself the opportunity to quickly sift through all the relevant material online and only collect what's most important. You then proceed to write from this consolidated, hyper-relevant collection of notes and source material. The benefit is that you can focus 100% on researching, and then 100% on writing, rather than having to mix both throughout the entire process. This tip alone is worth the cost of the book!

Now, before you go off and start researching the first topic that grabs your interest, you should figure out whether people are actually reading what it is you want to write about it.

Unfortunately, being an author does work in the Field of Dream sense of "if you build it, they will come." The same is true of business. A good product will satisfy the demands of the marketplace, rather than trying to manufacture demand by giving people things or information they don't already have (unless you have a brilliant marketing campaign that shows them exactly why they want what you have!).

With that in mind, here are two useful, free gauges of whether your book is poised for profit:

Free Research Resource #3: Amazon

Whether you are looking to publish your book on Amazon KDP (Kindle Direct Publishing), using Amazon's database of previously published books on any particular subject will help you immensely.

When you go Amazon.com, to the left of where you can type in search terms, you'll see the world word "all" directly next to an arrow pointing down. Click on that tab and scroll down to 'Kindle Store.'

Now, type in your topic or something specific to see what other books are already on Amazon.

Here's an extra tip: if you buy KindleUnlimited, you can scan through all of these books to see what they include, how they're formatted, and what's missing for you to talk about.

Even if you don't want to buy these books or invest in KindleUnlimited, you can usually 'Look Inside' any of the books to view a brief, selected portion of what's written.

Free Research Resource #4: Aggregator Websites

When you're struggling to figure out exactly how to package your book for the public's interest, there are aggregator websites like http://Digg.com and http://Reddit.com that list all of the most popular stories and posts from around the Internet.

Similarly, sites such as Twitter, Facebook, BuzzFeed, Huffington Post, New York Times, etc. all tell you 'what's trending' and what people are paying attention to.

With this information, you could gear your book toward an upcoming national holiday, high-profile media event, or really anything that's trending online.

CHAPTER 2: The 48-Hour Blueprint For Writing Your Book

"Don't be afraid it won't be perfect, be afraid that it won't be." ~Dean Jones

Here's where things get exciting.

Although I'm going to outline the process from square one, please keep in mind the extra details outlined in chapter 1 and what will be covered in chapter 3.

The point of this short chapter is to illustrate just how easy it can be to write *any book* on *any subject*, provided you have the time and motivation. The outline works for anything, including the books that *are already within you.*

For clarity, the example will start at 1 p.m. on a Monday and end at 1 p.m. on Wednesday.

Monday, 1 p.m. (hour 0)

Set the timer for 10 minutes.

Sit down at your computer and look over the aggregate websites, trending topics, and upcoming holidays or media events to see if there is anything that particularly grabs your interest.

If there is something that jumps out at you, claim it as your topic.

Get excited! For the sake of keeping things congruent, take a 5 minute celebration break.

Monday, 1:10 p.m.

If nothing caught your eye, go through Exercise #1 provided in Chapter 1.

Generate your own idea in 5 minutes.

Monday, 1:15 p.m

Begin your research.

Set a timer for 40 minutes and type in your desired topic into Google.

Open and save a new word document entitled '[Topic] Research.'

Going one piece of content at a time, copy/paste the highlights of what you're reading underneath the bolded URL and title heading.

40 minutes should take you through Google's first page, if not more. Avoid the Wikipedia article for now if it shows up in these immediate results.

Monday, 1:55 p.m.

Read through the Wikipedia article and at least half of the listed relevant resources, still keeping all the information tidily organized under bolded URL/title headings.

I'll give you, on a bad day, 65 minutes for this task.

Monday, 3 p.m. (hour 2)

Go through Amazon's eBook directory. Get a glimpse of what people are writing.

Make sure to read snippets of any best-sellers in your desired niche. Take note of the cover art, the titles, and the content. Copy/paste any compelling phrases or perspectives, since the feature is available when previewing Kindle books.

Again, keep everything clear and organized in your document, so that you can either easily navigate back to what you're referencing in the document or what you're writing makes sense by itself.

I'll give you another hour for this task.

Monday, 4 p.m. (hour 3)

Type in '[Topic] quotes' into Google and start collecting your favorites.

Create a list of at least 10.

As you can see using this book as an example, some quotes start each chapter and others are used to reference what a person said as a way to emphasize a certain point. Look back to the introduction for an example with John Wooden.

Take another hour for this task. Getting the right quotes can be very important, and can help shape the way you think about a topic.

Monday, 5 p.m. (hour 4)

Figure out the 5-10 most pressing questions that people are asking about your topic.

A few easy ways to accomplish this task are to type in either '[Topic] forum]' or '[Topic] blog' or '[Topic] FAQ.'

Take another hour to figure out which questions you are ready and able to answer.

Monday, 6.pm. (hour 5)

Under each of these 'major questions,' write 3-4 'minor questions' that relate to and flesh out the answer to the major questions.

For example, when writing this book, I felt that the 'major questions' and 'minor questions' I could answer in 6,000 words were:

1) How do I discover and research a topic?
   a. How do I figure out what I want to write about?
   b. What free tools are available?
   c. What are some tips that will help me get started and stay organized?
   d. How do I know whether people will want to read what I write?
2) What's a quick, reliable way for me to write a book?
   a. Is there a blueprint or system I can follow without breaking the bank?
   b. What are some simple ways I can make it look professional and not like I just put something together in 48 hours?
   c. What makes a good introduction, chapter, and conclusion, respectively?
   d. How should I structure the book?
3) How can I do more with less work?
   a. How can I hire someone else to do the work I don't want to do without breaking the bank?
   b. Who can help me figure out what to do after the book is published?
   c. Where do I go for ideas on design, marketing, and even content for the books itself?

Take a step back and look at what I just wrote.

Do you realize that the answer to each 'major question' is a chapter?

Do you realize that the answer to each 'minor question' is a sub-heading or point of discussion in each chapter?

Do you see how approaching your forthcoming book in this manner provides you with a powerful outline and an organized structure to present your information?

I hope so.

If you followed the instructions up to this point, you are at the 6th hour (assuming this last part took you 60 minutes), and you have:
- Decided on a topic
- Completed virtually all of your research
- Gathered information from Amazon about what's already selling and why
- Compiled a list of quotes
- Created an outline

6 hours in and you're ready to start writing!

Not bad, huh? Take a 30 minute break to eat dinner and refresh your mind.

Monday, 7:30 p.m.

Close everything out besides your research document. Create a dedicated space and time for you to write this book. Create a new document and title it '[Topic] eBook.'

A quick word to the wise: save your introduction and conclusion for last until you get good at writing these books consistently. Just trust me before you spend hours writing an intro just to rewrite it later because it repeats the content of the actual book.

Start with Chapter 1's 'major' and 'minor' questions. Paste them into your writing document.

Look through your research document and copy/paste over the relevant information and quotes that answer each question. Revisit the site or source of content if need be.

Once you've compiled a pretty hefty amount of researched information answering each question, it's time for you to add your personal answer to each question. After all, that's why you're writing the book, right?

Set a timer for 5 minutes for each 'major' and 'minor' question. Take a 30-second break in between each 5 minute chunk.

Now, similar to how you wrote stream-of-consciousness to generate a topic, you will write a continuous stream of thoughts and talking points that represent how you'd answer each question.

Once you've finished answering all the questions, take a break until the top of the hour.

Monday, 8 p.m. (hour 7)

Set your timer for 60 minutes.

You have one hour to write the first draft of your first chapter.

Trust me, if you set your mind to the task and keep your fingers on the keyboard the entire time, then 1 hour is plenty.

Take a 30 minute break.

Monday, 9:30 p.m. (hour 8)

Repeat the process for all the chapters in your book. Let's assume you have 4.

That would be 30 minutes to answer each chapter's questions, an hour to write the rough draft, and another 30 minutes for a break. That's 120 minutes (2 hours) total for each of the next 3 chapters.

Overall, that's another 6 hours.

Let's say that you slept for 8 hours at any point in time during this process.

That would put us at…

Tuesday, 11:30 a.m. (hour 22)

Now that you've created the rough version of your entire book, it's time to delve into the introduction and conclusion.

Aristotle actually shaped my thinking about how to structure the whole book: "Tell them what you are going to tell them, tell them, then tell them what you told them."

In the introduction, you 'tell them what you are going to tell them.'

In the chapters, you 'tell them.'

In the conclusion, you 'tell them what you told them.'

Although this is the basic concept, there are a few caveats I would add.

The first is that in the introduction you want to mention not only the underlying problem or question that urged you to write the book, but also the deeper problem that your book plans to solve.

For instance, if you look back to the introduction and the 'major' and 'minor' questions, you'll see that the problem I'm helping people with is 'How to Write a Non-Fiction Kindle eBook.' But, the deeper problem that people don't realize is that they are grappling with low self-esteem.

By presenting a deeper problem, I can also present a broader range of more powerful benefits, such as having the first book you publish be the foundation for a 6- or 7-figure online business.

The second caveat is that both your introduction and conclusion must have specific, clear Calls To Action (CTA).

You must tell the reader exactly what to expect and exactly what to do in order to achieve those things. Remove all room for doubt or confusion.

Give yourself another 60 minutes to write the introduction. Take a 30 minute break and return for another hour to write your conclusion. Then take another 30 minute break.

Tuesday, 2:30 p.m. (hour 25)

Hey! Just over a day and you've already completed your rough draft!

The method to this quick-paced madness is that you've taken all of the knowledge you gathered, put it on the page, and done it in a way where you write the most number of words possible in the shortest amount of time.

As I've said so many times before, you already have this book inside of you and by putting yourself through this strenuous time-crunching process, you limit your ability to critically analyze every word, phrase, and sentence structure.

You focus first on the bigger picture and getting your thoughts and voice down on to the page in the purest, most direct way possible. Only then do you come back through and refine the words into something ready for the public's eye.

So, first, what I want you to do is take 30 minutes to re-read everything you've written. Avoid specifically editing at this point in time. You'll get to that later.

Just bask in the glory of what you've written for a moment and really take in the overall message you're sending.

Tuesday, 3:00 p.m. (hour 26)

Time yourself for another hour for each part of the book: introduction, 4 chapters, and conclusion. Give yourself a 30 minute break in between.

At 90 minutes each for 6 sections, that would total 9 hours. Let's say you took another 8 hours to sleep at some point.

That would bring us to…

Wednesday, 8 a.m. (hour 43)

At this point, your book should basically be done.

Read through it one more time just to make sure you've caught all the typos, grammatical errors, and formatting mistakes.

Now, you're almost ready to publish onto Kindle Direct Publishing.

At some point during these last 43 hours, you should have contacted and hired someone to design your eBook's cover art. Exactly where to find people willing to help you with this task is the topic of the next chapter.

Assuming you have the design already, go the Amazon's Kindle Direct Publishing site. https://kdp.amazon.com.

You now have 5 hours to go through the process of uploading your book and having Amazon confirm its use on the KDP virtual bookshelves.

Congratulations!

CHAPTER 3: Outsourcing Guide

"For everything we don't like to do, there's someone out there who's really good, wants to do it and will enjoy it." ~Josh Kaufman

There's a nearly 100% chance that somewhere along the assembly line of writing a book, designing the cover, and having that act as the business card for your 6- or 7- figure business, you are going to face some areas where you are weak.

Maybe you aren't an expert at Photoshop.

Maybe sales and marketing aren't your things.

Or maybe it's the admin side of the business that could use a helping hand.

In any case, as Josh Kaufman points out, there are people you can hire that will enjoy picking up the slack on the parts of this process where you're weak.

Now, maybe you don't want to hire a part- or full-time employee, but are still seeking professional solutions.

Don't worry because so many other companies have felt the same way that in recent years websites dedicated to remotely connecting specialists with employers have sprouted and thrived.

Here is a break down of some of the most powerful for you, even if you're just writing a book.

oDesk.com and Elance.com

Although these two sites are separate, the umbrella companies have merged.

You'll find that the concepts and the opportunities are similar on both sites, so it's fair to clump them.

On either of these freelancing sites, you can create an employer account and post a job with the specifics about what you're looking for.

You post the budget, estimated numbers of hours, and a brief description of what kind of work you're looking to get done.

Within minutes you'll receive bids from around the world from a range of freelancers. Some are experts, who charge the highest rates but might be the most valuable for your team. Others are cheap and reliable.

The best part is that each freelancer has a profile complete with work history, average feedback score, and emphasized skills.

99Designs.com

99 Designs started in 2008 and quickly became a hot spot for employers looking for high-quality design work.

The site is stacked heavily in favor of the employer due to how the process works.

When you post a design project, a large number of designers will each submit their unique version of what would fit for your request.

You get to pick and pay for only the winner.

Fiverr.com

This site is similar to oDesk and Elance in that it connects employers with freelancers worldwide for virtually every different kind of job opportunity.

The benefit and potential consequence of Fiverr is that every job is strictly $5, disregarding the potential 'extras,' such as fast delivery, special requests, and revision.

You could potentially get a book cover designed for $5, but I want to re-emphasize that revisions and corrections typically cost more.

The fundamental insight from learning about these websites is that you can outsource everything these days.

If you didn't want to write your own book, you could even outsource a ghostwriter to help!

For those of you who are hesitant about outsourcing and what that might do to your business, just remember the words of Azim Premji, "the important thing about outsourcing or global sourcing is that it becomes a very powerful tool to leverage talent, improve productivity and reduce work cycles."

Just because you *can* do everything by yourself (which is becoming more and more unlikely in our technical age), doesn't mean that you *should*.

You and your business will benefit greatly by including other people, even if they work remotely, who balance out your weaknesses.

Through these freelance websites, you now have the opportunity to streamline the recruitment process from a range of professionals *from everywhere around the world.*

It doesn't get much better than that!

Conclusion

Thank you, and thank yourself, for taking the time to read this short book!

You now have the power to turn an idea into money within a couple days, which is a powerful skill to have in business and in life.

If you can crank out a book in 48 hours, then you can constantly provide relevant, useful information to people on an on-going basis.

You can feed off of hyped events like March Madness, the Super Bowl, and holidays.

You can publish a book right before Thanksgiving or Christmas explaining the roots of the traditions or recipes that will appeal to the whole family.

You can publish a book right after the occasions to ride the wave of the media attention and capture the portion of the public who's still interested.

The main takeaway from this book is that *you can write whatever you want.*

You are now equipped with the blueprint, the resources, and hopefully the motivation to capitalize on the amazing opportunity sitting right in front you.

The Internet has forever changed how people create, sustain, and innovate their businesses.

With one machine, you can access the Internet, compile all your research, write the entire book, and publish it to on a platform that will reach everyone, everywhere, forever. Yes, once you publish an eBook on Amazon, it will stay up on the site until the Internet dies.

In fact, one commonly overlooked benefit to publishing a valuable eBook on Amazon is residual income.

Let's think about this for a second.

Have you ever bought a product on Amazon?

When you did, did you talk to a company representative?

Did you need anything other than the reviews and description on the site to decide whether to buy?

Most likely not.

Thus, in this same way, once you start publishing Amazon Kindle books, you will start to make money *as you sleep* because these books are now instantly accessible to everyone with Internet access, 24/7.

That means even 5, 25, or even 55 years from now, someone could find your book, buy it, and you still make money! The best part is that Amazon, the reviews, and your credibility will do all the selling for you!

Think about if you wrote 100 of these books over the next 2-3 years.

What would that do for your income and quality of life?

What would that do for your credibility and business?

What would that do for your levels of self-esteem?

Let me tell you from personal experience that taking the time to investigate what you're passionate about and learning how to communicate those ideas effectively to other people will act as a turning point in your life.

You will no longer have to worry about clearly expressing your complicated ideas about Mutually Assured Destruction or Nixon's Impeachment in the heat of the moment. You can just point people to your book, or send them a free copy.

Over time, you will become more decisive, more powerful, richer, happier, and, most important, have higher self-esteem.

You will be immersed in your ocean of wisdom and knowledge, rather than suppressing and burying it in a tiny well.

In other words, you will tap into the incredible resources that are already at your fingertips but have only seemed inaccessible due to your beliefs and assumptions.

With all that being said, I want to thank you again for taking the time to read this book all the way through.

Conclusion

Thank you again for downloading this book!

I hope this book was able to help you to overcome the emotional neglect that you experienced as a child. Many of us believe that we will never overcome poor rearing practices until we are presented with ways to deal with the past and move towards the future. It is my hope that this book has helped you do that.

The next step in the process is to determine how you would like to progress. What are your goals in life, and how can you make these dreams your reality?

Before you go, I'd like to say thank you for purchasing my book.

I know you could have picked so many other books to read on writing a kindle ebook. .But you took a chance on me.

So A Big thanks for downloading this book and reading it all the way to completion.

Now I would like to ask a _small_ favor.

Could you please take a minute or two to leave a review for this book on Amazon?

Click here

The feedback will help me continue to publish more kindle books that will help people to get better results in their lives.

And if you found it helpful in anyway then please let me know :-)

Thank you and good luck!

To your success,

Michele

Preview of My New Book..

Adrenal Fatigue
What Is Adrenal Fatigue Syndrome And How To Reset Your Diet And Your Life

CHAPTER 1
So What Is Adrenal Fatigue

Get used to the idea right away that even if your symptoms fit like a glove, a good many people, including doctors, may tell you there is no such thing as Adrenal Fatigue. There are illnesses which share the symptoms, and you should rule those out first. The chances are, though, that you have picked this book because you've had all the tests, you've been cleared as healthy—and yet you still feel as though healthy and active is a dim and distant memory. The best thing to do next is learn as much as you can about Adrenal Fatigue. You picked the right book!

The following sections are designed to tell you the symptoms and causes of the syndrome, those likeliest to have it, the lifestyle triggers for it (and managing or changing them), the traditional and homeopathic approaches, adjusting your diet, and ways of tackling the problem generally. One thing is for sure, nothing in this book can do other than help. That's important, because some of the supplements and vitamins marketed to treat Adrenal Fatigue aren't necessarily safe, and can have the opposite effect, causing your adrenal glands more distress. Treatments can also be expensive, because medical insurance won't usually cover them.

Before you could skip straight to the next section, with the signs and symptoms, you should learn what adrenal fatigue is.

The adrenal glands are walnut-sized, situated above each kidney, and react swiftly to help you cope with difficult situations. They were originally designed to flood our systems with the boost we needed in emergencies, but the problem with modern life is that the brain is constantly reacting to what it sees as emergency situations. Stress, handled properly, is actually essential to our survival but when the button is pressed too often, triggering a body response time and again, the glands go into overdrive, or they malfunction.

There are two of them and when they are working normally they provide, in lay terms, adrenaline (the fight-or-flight hormone), noradrenaline (which reacts to fear and affects blood pressure), cortisol (which plays a role in blood sugar management and your immune system) dopamine (affecting your nervous central system) and steroids. They are essential to our wellbeing and balance. Healthy adrenal gland secretions have us feeling at our strongest and most alert at the start of the day, tapering off naturally towards the end of the day, so that we fall asleep easily, wake feeling rested, and have energy to call on.

Constant or intense stress, or respiratory infections, even a serious attack of 'flu, can affect their performance and leave you feeling tired, unwell, depressed and generally off-color. When this gray feeling can't be shaken off and becomes chronic, yet medical tests can't pick up any physical cause, you have a classic Adrenal Fatigue profile. It probably isn't any consolation, but you share that profile with millions of others.

CHAPTER 2
What Are The Signs And Symptoms Of Adrenal Fatigue

It has been referred to as the 21st century stress disorder, and is often dismissed by the medical profession. In fairness to them, changes to the adrenal glands can be too slight to be picked up in medical tests, despite the impact even slight changes have to the body. To anyone suffering it, the changes may be medically slight, but they have a devastating effect on lifestyle, especially as it often affects people who eat healthily, exercise, and keep themselves in shape, yet are increasingly fatigued.

If you have several of the following symptoms, there are tests that will pick up the more alarming alternatives, listed at the end of this section. Have them done.

Click here to read the rest of…
Adrenal Fatigue
What Is Adrenal Fatigue Syndrome And How To Reset Your Diet And Your Life

P.S. You'll find many more books like this and others under my name Michele Gilbert.

Don't miss them… here is a short list.

Wicca: The Ultimate Beginners Guide For Witches and Warlocks: Learn Wicca Magic

The Introvert's Advantage: The Introverts Guide To Succeeding In An Extrovert World

Stop Playing Mind Games: How To Free Yourself Of Controlling And Manipulating Relationships

Instant Charisma: A Quick And Easy Guide To Talk, Impress, And Make Anyone Like You

Chakras: Understanding The 7 Main Chakras For Beginners: The Ultimate Guide To Chakra Mindfulness, Balance and Healing

Practicing Mindfulness: Living in the moment through Meditation: Everyday Habits and Rituals to help you achieve inner peace

Adrenal Fatigue: What Is Adrenal Fatigue Syndrome And How To Reset Your Diet And Your Life

Sleep Tight: Overcome Insomnia and Sleep Disorders for a better more restful sleep!

Stop Back Pain Now!: Back Pain Remedies and Treatments so you can live a pain free life!

The Arthritis Pain Cure: How to find Arthritis Pain Relief and live a happy pain free life!

The Headache Pain Cure: How to find Headache Pain Relief and live a happy Pain Free Life!

Stop Panic Attacks and Anxiety Disorders without Drugs Now!: Overcome Panic, Stress and Anxiety and live a happy pain free life!

The Breakup Recovery Guide: Advice for Surviving Heartbreak, Letting Go and Thriving in an exciting new life!

The Friendship Guide to Finding Friends Forever: How to Find, Make and Keep Quality Friendships After your Breakup

The Credit Fix: Leave behind credit card debt and poor credit scores and get your life back!

How To Stop Being Jealous And Insecure: Overcome Insecurity And Relationship Jealousy

So I Am Dating A Psycopath: Now What?

Michele Gilbert was born and raised in Brooklyn, New York. Drawn to literature and writing at a young age, she enrolled at Brooklyn College and majored in English. After graduation Michele did not begin writing immediately, instead she embarked on a career in the finance industry and spent the next thirty years on Wall Street.

Serendipity struck when she least expected it. After ending a long-term relationship, Michele found herself lost and unsure what the future held. She began to read books on grief and loss, looking for answers. Those led her to delve deeper into the Law of Attraction and its power. What resulted was remarkable. Not only had she begun to heal, she had also rekindled her former love of writing and discovered her life's purpose.

The years have taken her through many twists and turns, but she learned valuable lessons along the way. Today she publishes books-mostly self-help and metaphysical in nature-and feels compelled to share her knowledge with those facing similar experiences. Her greatest hope is to inspire others and show them ways to overcome adversity and gracefully accept life's inevitable low points.

Going forward, she plans to incorporate more teachings of self-help, finance and meditation. Regular meditation is very beneficial to her progress as she forges a new life. Morning rituals and positive incantations are other practices Michele embraces; they are very restorative in daily life.

As an avid hiker, Michele and fellow club members often hike the picturesque Jersey Pine Barrens. She is a history buff, voracious reader, baseball fanatic and a foodie. She also proudly supports Trout Unlimited-a national non-profit organization dedicated to conserving, protecting and restoring North America's Coldwater fisheries and their watersheds.

Michele currently resides forty minutes from Atlantic City and the Jersey Shore. She makes her home with a Blue Russian rescue cat named Jersey, though she isn't exactly sure who rescued who.

Michele really enjoys publishing books that can make a difference in people's lives. If you have any suggestions or would like to have a specific topic covered in a future book, please send an email to michelegilbertbooks@gmail.com and we will get back to you.

Thanks for reading!